Contents

Cheesy Tuna Noodle Casserole..4

Beef & Rice Taco Casserole 6

Homestyle Chicken & Biscuits...8

Broccoli & Cheese Casserole..10

Chicken Noodle Casserole...12

Sloppy Joe Casserole 14

Three Cheese Baked Ziti with Spinach 16

Hearty Chicken & Noodle Casserole............................ 18

Beef and Mozzarella Bake.. 20

Cheesy Chicken & Rice Casserole................................ 22

Garlic Mashed Potatoes & Beef Bake.........................24

Chicken Broccoli Divan 26

Baked Macaroni & Cheese...27

Monterey Chicken Tortilla Casserole 28

Creamy 3-Cheese Pasta 29

Tuna Noodle Casserole.. 30

Cheesy Tuna Noodle Casserole

Makes 4 servings

Prep Time: 10 minutes   *Bake Time: 22 minutes*

1 can (10³/₄ ounces) Campbell's® Condensed Cream of Mushroom Soup (Regular *or* 98% Fat Free)

¹/₂ cup milk

1 cup frozen peas

2 cans (about 6 ounces *each*) tuna, drained and flaked

2 cups hot cooked medium egg noodles

¹/₂ cup shredded Cheddar cheese

1. Stir the soup, milk, peas, tuna and noodles in a 1¹/₂-quart casserole.

2. Bake at 400°F. for 20 minutes or until hot. Stir.

3. Sprinkle cheese over the tuna mixture. Bake for 2 minutes more or until the cheese melts.

Kitchen Tip

Substitute your family's favorite frozen vegetable for the peas.

Beef & Rice Taco Casserole

Makes 4 servings

Prep Time: 10 minutes   Bake Time: 25 minutes

- 1 pound ground beef
- 1 can (10^3/$_4$ ounces) Campbell's® Condensed Tomato Soup (Regular *or* Healthy Request®)
- 1 cup Pace® Picante Sauce
- ^{1}/$_2$ cup milk
- ^{1}/$_2$ cup **uncooked** instant white rice
- ^{1}/$_2$ cup crushed tortilla chips
- ^{1}/$_2$ cup shredded Cheddar cheese

1. Cook the beef in a 10-inch skillet over medium-high heat until the beef is well browned, stirring frequently to separate meat. Pour off any fat.

2. Stir the soup, picante sauce, milk and rice into the skillet. Spoon the soup mixture into a 1^1/$_2$-quart casserole. Cover the dish with foil.

3. Bake at 400°F. for 25 minutes or until hot. Stir.

4. Sprinkle the chips around the edge of the casserole. Sprinkle with the cheese.

Homestyle Chicken & Biscuits

Makes 4 servings

Prep Time: **15 minutes**   *Bake Time:* **30 minutes**

- 1 can (10 ³/₄ ounces) Campbell's® Condensed Cream of Chicken Soup (Regular *or* 98% Fat Free)
- ¹/₄ cup milk
- ³/₄ cup shredded Cheddar cheese
- ¹/₄ teaspoon ground black pepper
- 1 bag (16 ounces) frozen vegetable combination (broccoli, cauliflower, carrots), thawed
- 2 cans (4.5 ounces *each*) Swanson® Premium Chunk Chicken Breast in Water, drained
- 1 package (7.5 ounces) refrigerated biscuits (10 biscuits)

1. Heat the oven to 400°F. Stir the soup, milk, cheese and black pepper in a 3-quart shallow baking dish. Stir in the vegetables and chicken.

2. Bake for 15 minutes or until the chicken mixture is hot and bubbling. Stir the chicken mixture.

3. Top the chicken mixture with the biscuits. Bake for 15 minutes or until the biscuits are golden brown.

Kitchen Tip

Use the downtime while this one-dish meal is in the oven to make a fresh tomato salad: slice some tomatoes and drizzle them with balsamic vinegar and olive oil.

Broccoli & Cheese Casserole

Makes 6 servings

Prep Time: 10 minutes   Bake Time: 30 minutes

1 can (10^3/$_4$ ounces) Campbell's® Condensed Cream of Mushroom Soup (Regular *or* 98% Fat Free)

^{1}/$_2$ cup milk

2 teaspoons yellow mustard

1 bag (16 ounces) frozen broccoli flowerets, thawed

1 cup shredded Cheddar cheese (about 4 ounces)

^{1}/$_3$ cup dry bread crumbs

2 teaspoons butter, melted

1. Stir the soup, milk, mustard, broccoli and cheese in a 1^1/$_2$-quart casserole.

2. Mix the bread crumbs with the butter in a small bowl. Sprinkle the crumb mixture over the broccoli mixture.

3. Bake at 350°F. for 30 minutes or until the mixture is hot and bubbling.

Rice Is Nice: Add **2 cups** cooked white rice to the broccoli mixture before baking.

Cheese Change-Up: Substitute mozzarella cheese for Cheddar.

Chicken Noodle Casserole

Makes 4 servings

Prep Time: **10 minutes**   *Bake Time:* **25 minutes**

> 1 can (10$^3/_4$ ounces) Campbell's® Condensed Cream of Mushroom Soup (Regular *or* 98% Fat Free)

$^1/_2$ cup milk

2 tablespoons butter, melted

$^1/_4$ teaspoon ground black pepper

1 cup frozen broccoli flowerets, thawed

2 cups shredded cooked chicken

2 cups hot cooked medium egg noodles

$^1/_2$ cup grated Parmesan cheese

1. Stir soup, milk, butter, black pepper, broccoli, chicken and noodles in a 2-quart casserole.

2. Bake at 400°F. for 20 minutes or until hot. Stir.

3. Sprinkle with the cheese. Bake for 5 minutes more.

Sloppy Joe Casserole

Makes 5 servings

Prep Time: 15 minutes   Bake Time: 15 minutes

- 1 pound ground beef
- 1 can (10 $^3/_4$ ounces) Campbell's® Condensed Tomato Soup (Regular *or* Healthy Request®)
- $^1/_4$ cup water
- 1 teaspoon Worcestershire sauce
- $^1/_8$ teaspoon ground black pepper
- 1 package (7.5 ounces) refrigerated biscuits (10 biscuits)
- $^1/_2$ cup shredded Cheddar cheese

1. Heat the oven to 400°F.

2. Cook the beef in a 10-inch skillet over medium-high heat until it's well browned, stirring often to separate meat. Pour off any fat.

3. Stir the soup, water, Worcestershire and black pepper in the skillet and heat to a boil. Spoon the beef mixture into a 1$^1/_2$-quart casserole. Arrange the biscuits around the inside edge of the casserole.

4. Bake for 15 minutes or until the biscuits are golden brown. Sprinkle the cheese over the beef mixture.

Kitchen Tip

Sharp **or** *mild Cheddar cheese will work in this recipe.*

Three Cheese Baked Ziti with Spinach

Makes 6 servings

Prep Time: 15 minutes   Bake Time: 30 minutes

1 box (16 ounces) medium tube-shaped pasta (ziti)

1 bag (6 ounces) baby spinach leaves (4 cups), washed

1 jar (1 pound 9 ounces) Prego® Marinara Italian Sauce

1 cup ricotta cheese

1 cup shredded mozzarella cheese (4 ounces)

$3/4$ cup grated Parmesan cheese

$1/2$ teaspoon garlic powder

$1/4$ teaspoon ground black pepper

1. Prepare the pasta according to the package directions. Add the spinach during the last minute of the cooking time. Drain the pasta and spinach well in a colander. Return them to the saucepot.

2. Stir the Italian sauce, ricotta, *$1/2$ cup* of the mozzarella cheese, *$1/2$ cup* of the Parmesan cheese, garlic powder and black pepper into the pasta mixture. Spoon the pasta mixture into a 13×9×2-inch shallow baking dish. Sprinkle with the remaining mozzarella and Parmesan cheeses.

3. Bake at 350°F. for 30 minutes or until hot and bubbling.

Kitchen Tip

Prepare through step 2. Cover and refrigerate up to 6 hours. Uncover and let come to room temperature before baking.

Hearty Chicken & Noodle Casserole

Makes 4 servings

Prep Time: 15 minutes   Bake Time: 25 minutes

1 can (10³/₄ ounces) Campbell's® Condensed Cream of Mushroom Soup (Regular *or* 98% Fat Free)

¹/₂ cup milk

¹/₄ teaspoon ground black pepper

1 cup frozen mixed vegetables

2 cups cubed cooked chicken

¹/₄ of a 12-ounce package medium egg noodles (about 2 cups), cooked and drained

¹/₄ cup grated Parmesan cheese

¹/₂ cup shredded Cheddar cheese

1. Heat the oven to 400°F. Stir the soup, milk, black pepper, vegetables, chicken, noodles and Parmesan cheese in a 1¹/₂-quart casserole.

2. Bake for 25 minutes or until the chicken mixture is hot and bubbling. Stir the chicken mixture. Top with the Cheddar cheese.

Kitchen Tip

*Easy casseroles like this one are a simple way to transform leftovers. Cooked chicken, turkey **or** ham will all work in this recipe.*

Beef and Mozzarella Bake

Makes 6 servings

Prep Time: 10 minutes   Bake Time: 25 minutes

- 1 pound ground beef
- 1 teaspoon dried basil leaves, crushed
- $1/4$ teaspoon ground black pepper
- $1/8$ teaspoon garlic powder *or* 1 clove garlic, minced
- $1^1/4$ cups Prego® Traditional Italian Sauce
- 1 can (10$^3/4$ ounces) Campbell's® Condensed Cream of Mushroom Soup (Regular *or* 98% Fat Free)
- $1^1/4$ cups water
- $1^1/2$ cups shredded mozzarella cheese (6 ounces)
- 3 cups medium shell-shaped pasta, cooked and drained

1. Cook the beef, basil, black pepper and garlic powder in a 10-inch skillet over medium-high heat until well browned, stirring frequently to separate meat. Pour off any fat.

2. Stir the Italian sauce, soup, water and **1 cup** of the mozzarella cheese into the skillet. Stir in the pasta to coat with the sauce mixture. Spoon into a 2-quart shallow baking dish. Sprinkle with the remaining cheese.

3. Bake at 400°F. for 25 minutes or until hot and bubbling.

Cheesy Chicken & Rice Casserole

Makes 4 servings

Prep Time: 15 minutes   *Bake Time: 50 minutes*   *Stand Time: 10 minutes*

1 can (10³/₄ ounces) Campbell's® Condensed Cream of Chicken Soup (Regular *or* 98% Fat Free)

1¹/₃ cups water

³/₄ cup **uncooked** regular long-grain white rice

¹/₂ teaspoon onion powder

¹/₄ teaspoon ground black pepper

2 cups frozen mixed vegetables

4 skinless, boneless chicken breast halves

¹/₂ cup shredded Cheddar cheese

1. Heat the oven to 375°F. Stir the soup, water, rice, onion powder, black pepper and vegetables in a 2-quart shallow baking dish.

2. Top with the chicken. Season the chicken as desired. Cover the baking dish.

3. Bake for 50 minutes or until the chicken is cooked through and the rice is tender. Top with the cheese. Let the casserole stand for 10 minutes. Stir the rice before serving.

Kitchen Tip

*To try it Alfredo: Substitute broccoli flowerets for the vegetables and substitute ¹/₄ **cup** grated Parmesan for the Cheddar cheese. Add **2 tablespoons** Parmesan cheese with the soup. Sprinkle the chicken with the remaining Parmesan cheese.*

Trim It Down: Use Campbell's® 98% Fat Free Condensed Cream of Chicken Soup instead of regular soup and use low-fat cheese instead of regular cheese.

Mexican: In place of onion powder and pepper use **1 teaspoon** chili powder. Substitute Mexican cheese blend for Cheddar.

Italian: In place of onion powder and pepper use **1 teaspoon** Italian seasoning, crushed. Substitute ⅓ **cup** shredded Parmesan for Cheddar.

Garlic Mashed Potatoes & Beef Bake

Makes 4 servings

Prep Time: 15 minutes   Bake Time: 20 minutes

1 pound ground beef

1 can (10 3/4 ounces) Campbell's® Condensed Cream of Mushroom with Roasted Garlic Soup

1 tablespoon Worcestershire sauce

1 bag (16 ounces) frozen vegetable combination (broccoli, cauliflower, carrots), thawed

2 cups water

3 tablespoons butter

3/4 cup milk

2 cups instant mashed potato flakes

1. Heat the oven to 400°F. Cook the beef in a 10-inch skillet over medium-high heat until it's well browned, stirring often to separate meat. Pour off any fat.

2. Stir the beef, 1/2 **can** soup, Worcestershire and vegetables in a 2-quart shallow baking dish.

3. Heat the water, butter and remaining soup in a 3-quart saucepan over medium heat to a boil. Remove the saucepan from the heat. Stir in the milk. Stir in the potatoes. Spoon the potatoes over the beef mixture.

4. Bake for 20 minutes or until the potatoes are lightly browned.

Kitchen Tip

You can use your favorite frozen vegetable combination in this recipe.

Chicken Broccoli Divan

Makes 4 servings

Prep Time: 10 minutes   Bake Time: 20 minutes

    4 cups cooked broccoli flowerets
1$^1/_2$ cups cubed cooked chicken
    1 can (10$^3/_4$ ounces) Campbell's® Condensed Cream of Chicken Soup
       (Regular *or* 98% Fat Free)
 $^1/_3$ cup milk
 $^1/_2$ cup shredded Cheddar cheese
    2 tablespoons dry bread crumbs
    1 tablespoon butter, melted

1. Heat the oven to 450°F. Place the broccoli and chicken into a 9-inch deep-dish pie plate.

2. Stir the soup and milk in a small bowl. Pour the soup mixture over the broccoli and chicken. Sprinkle with the cheese. Stir the bread crumbs and butter in a small bowl. Sprinkle the bread crumbs over the cheese.

3. Bake for 20 minutes or until the cheese is melted and the bread crumbs are golden brown.

Kitchen Tip

You can use leftover cooked turkey instead of the chicken in this recipe.

Baked Macaroni & Cheese

Makes 4 servings

Prep Time: **20 minutes**   **Bake Time:** **20 minutes**

1 can (10³/₄ ounces) Campbell's® Condensed Cheddar Cheese Soup

¹/₂ soup can milk

¹/₈ teaspoon ground black pepper

1¹/₂ cups corkscrew **or** medium shell-shaped pasta, cooked and drained

1 tablespoon dry bread crumbs

2 teaspoons butter, melted

1. Stir the soup, milk, black pepper and pasta in a 1-quart casserole.

2. Mix the bread crumbs with the butter in a small bowl. Sprinkle over the pasta mixture.

3. Bake at 400°F. for 20 minutes or until hot.

To Double Recipe: Double all ingredients, except increase butter to **1 tablespoon**, use 2-quart casserole and increase baking time to 25 minutes.

Variation: Substitute **2 cups** hot cooked elbow macaroni (about 1 cup **uncooked**) for corkscrew **or** shell-shaped pasta.

Monterey Chicken Tortilla Casserole

Makes 4 servings

Prep Time: 15 minutes   Bake Time: 40 minutes

- 1 cup coarsely crumbled tortilla chips
- 2 cups cubed cooked chicken *or* turkey
- 1 can (about 15 ounces) cream-style corn
- 3/4 cup Pace® Picante Sauce
- 1/2 cup sliced pitted ripe olives
- 2 ounces shredded Cheddar cheese (about 1/2 cup)

   Chopped green *or* red pepper

   Tortilla chips

1. Layer the crumbled chips, chicken, corn and picante sauce in a 1-quart casserole. Top with the olives and cheese.

2. Bake at 350°F. for 40 minutes or until the mixture is hot and bubbling. Top with the pepper. Serve with the chips.

Creamy 3-Cheese Pasta

Makes 4 servings

*Prep Time: 20 minutes**Bake Time: 20 minutes*

1 can (10³/₄ ounces) Campbell's® Condensed Cream of Mushroom Soup (Regular *or* 98% Fat Free)

1 cup milk

¹/₄ teaspoon ground black pepper

1 package (8 ounces) shredded two-cheese blend

¹/₃ cup grated Parmesan cheese

3 cups corkscrew-shaped pasta (rotelle), cooked and drained

1. Stir the soup, milk, black pepper and cheeses in a 1¹/₂-quart casserole dish. Stir in the pasta.

2. Bake at 400°F. for 20 minutes or until hot.

3. Stir before serving.

Tuna Noodle Casserole

Makes 8 servings

Prep Time: 10 minutes   Bake Time: 35 minutes

2 cans (10³/₄ ounces *each*) Campbell's® Condensed Cream of Mushroom Soup (Regular *or* 98% Fat Free)

1 cup milk

2 cups frozen peas

2 cans (about 10 ounces *each*) tuna, drained

¹/₂ of a 12-ounce package medium egg noodles (about 4 cups), cooked and drained

2 tablespoons dry bread crumbs

1 tablespoon butter, melted

1. Stir the soup, milk, peas, tuna and noodles in a 3-quart casserole.

2. Bake at 400°F. for 30 minutes or until the tuna mixture is hot and bubbling. Stir the tuna mixture.

3. Stir the bread crumbs and butter in a small bowl. Sprinkle the bread crumb mixture over the tuna mixture. Bake for 5 minutes or until the topping is golden brown.

Day is done.
Gone the sun
From the lake,
From the hills,
From the sky.
All is well,
Safely rest.
God is nigh.

Our Father, who art in Heaven,

Hallowed be Thy name.

Thy kingdom come,

Thy will be done

On earth as it is in Heaven.

Give us this day our daily bread,

And forgive us our trespasses

As we forgive those

Who trespass against us.

Lead us not into temptation,

But deliver us from evil.

For Thine is the kingdom,

And the power,

And the glory forever. Amen.

Sleep, my child, and peace attend thee
  All through the night.
Guardian angels God will send thee
  All through the night.

Soft the drowsy hours are creeping,
  Hill and vale in slumber sleeping,
While the moon her watch is keeping
  All through the night.

O'er thy spirit gently stealing,
  Visions of delight revealing,
Breathes a pure and holy feeling
  All through the night.

Jesus, friend of little children,
  Be a friend to me.
Take my hand and ever keep me
  Close to Thee.

Teach me how to grow in goodness
  Daily, as I grow.
Thou hast been a child,
  And surely Thou dost know.

Never leave me nor forsake me,
  Ever be my friend,
For I need Thee from life's dawning
  To its end.

Two little eyes to look to God,
Two little ears to hear His word.
Two little feet to walk in His ways,
Hands to serve Him all my days.

What can I give Him,
  Poor as I am?
If I were a shepherd,
  I would bring a lamb.
If I were a wise man,
  I would do my part.
But what can I give Him?
  I will give my heart.

All things bright and beautiful,
All creatures great and small,
All things wise and wonderful—
The Lord God made them all!

Each little flower that opens,
Each little bird that sings—
He made their glowing colors;
He made their tiny wings.

He gave us eyes to see them
And lips that we might tell
How great is God Almighty,
Who has made all things well!

God made the sun,
  And God made the trees.
God made the mountains,
  And God made me.

Thank you, O God,
  For the sun and the trees,
For making the mountains,
  And for making me.

I see the moon.
The moon sees me.
God bless the moon,
And God bless me.

God be in my head

    And in my thinking.

God be in my eyes

    And in my seeing.

God be in my mouth

    And in my speaking.

God be in my heart

    And in my understanding.

To do to others as I would

That they should do to me

Will make me gentle, kind, and good,

As children ought to be.

God is great,
And God is good.
Now we thank Him
For this food. Amen.

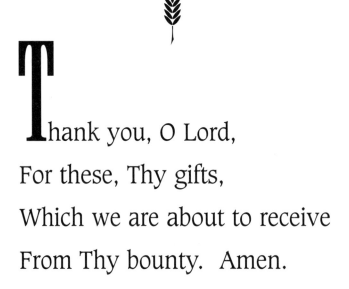

Thank you, O Lord,
For these, Thy gifts,
Which we are about to receive
From Thy bounty. Amen.

Thank you for the world so sweet,
Thank you for the food we eat.
Thank you for the birds that sing,
Thank you, God, for everything.

Dear Lord, teach this child to pray,
And then accept my prayer.
You hear all the words I say
For You are everywhere.